CW01021406

Contents

PERSONAL LINKS

Matteo Romano
- *Blog*
- *LinkedIn*

Hassan Elfadul
- *Instagram*
- *Spotify*

Eric Ries, *The Lean Startup: How Today's Entrepreneurs Use Continuous Innovation to Create Radically Successful Businesses*, 2011

Jordan Belfort, *Way of the Wolf: Straight Line Selling: Master the Art of Persuasion, Influence, and Success*, 2018

Robert G. Hagstrom, *The Warren Buffett Way*, 2013

Lextalk.com, *Optimizing Your LinkedIn Footprint: 8 Critical Tips For Your Career Success*, 2015

Medium.com, *Guide linkedin audience segmentation*, 2019

Linkedselling.com, *How to use advanced people search on linkedin*

Hubspot.com, *Buyer Persona Research*, 2020

Deloitte Touche Tohmatsu Limited, *Robotic Process Automation*,

Zety.com, *Job titles*, 2020

UiPath.com, *Roboti Process Automation*

Distruptiveadvertising,.com, *16 Content Ideas that Will Make You a LinkedIn Superstar*, 2019

CHAPTER:1
INTRODUCTION

1.1 LinkedIn: the B2B Precision Marketing platform

Have you ever thought about what is the **best strategy to reach targeted and precise B2B customers?** If you are reading this book it is probably because you realize the incredible potential that resides in LinkedIn and therefore you want to learn, improve the use of this incredible tool and generate potential customers for your business.

The main **problem** that many entrepreneurs and companies encounter does not lie so much in the service or product they offer to the public but rather lies in the ability to reach the right people at the right time and to be able to organize appointments with their ideal customers. It is in fact one of the main problems that the various marketing departments and sellers in any sector face every single day because you can also have a service of excellent quality that solves a specific customer problem but, if you are not able to achieve this blessed customer it is impossible to bill.

Nowadays, standard marketing strategies such as cold calling, events and traditional advertising are at a breaking point with the past. In fact, in such a fast-paced world, all professionals are required to make fast and efficient decisions so **it is no longer acceptable to spend excessive time calling a list of non-target contacts** for hours and hours, many times without even closing a deal.

It is no longer acceptable
to spend excessive time calling
a list of non-target contacts

It is necessary to **reinvent yourself and make use of all those modern and digital tools** that allow you to solve the same problem in a fraction of time.

I myself during my professional career had to face this problem and over time I managed to develop a strategy that allows me **to reach potential target customers in an easy, fast way** and that allows me to focus on the most important thing that is the negotiation.

This is a strategy that I have had the opportunity to implement both through my personal activity which I will talk about later, but also through those companies with which I have had the pleasure of collaborating and to which I hope to have contributed by adding value.

That is why one of the main tools that I use to promote my business and that of my customers is LinkedIn, which I learned to exploit and today I **appreciate its effectiveness** through which it allows you to develop business relationships with other companies.

All the people who are serious professionals are now on LinkedIn for the same reason as you: Business.

Given that LinkedIn is becoming so crucial and pervasive in the way we work every day, I believe that in the years to come LinkedIn will consolidate its leadership as business social media worldwide.

However, despite the fact that millions of users around the world check their LinkedIn page every day, many people still fail to use LinkedIn and exploit its full potential.

For many people including CEOs, general managers, CFOs, salespeople, entrepreneurs, freelancers, human resources departments and consultants, spending time on LinkedIn is frustrating. Why? Because they feel that they are spending time unnecessarily because their efforts receives zero results and eventually end the day by stating   that:

"LInkedIn is not working"

Or alternatively many people decide to invest disproportionate budgets in LinkedIn's paid marketing platform, achieving exactly the same results as the free version, that is: Zero.

But here is the news:
These failures constitute a great,
I say, huge opportunity for you.

If you follow the advice and guidance that I am here to provide you, you will be able to become a pro in the generation of leads through LinkedIn. You will organize meetings with potentially anyone.

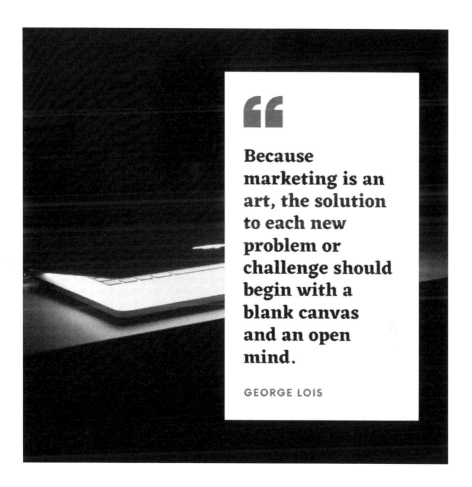

> **Because marketing is an art, the solution to each new problem or challenge should begin with a blank canvas and an open mind.**
>
> GEORGE LOIS

What we will specifically deal with in this book:

1. I will guide you in optimizing your profile in order to attract as many people as possible to your personal page and generate business opportunities passively

2. I will help you identify who your ideal customers are, to understand their behavior and to use LinkedIn to reach them effectively.

3. I will explain to you in detail the strategy that I have personally used to convert 15% of the people reached into new leads with my marketing strategy. I will provide you with the specific funnel that I have used, and a series of templates that have helped me during these years.

4. I will help you understand How to re-establish a relationship with those people who have never replied to your messages.

5. I will guide you in creating a LinkedIn group, a professional LinkedIn page, effective LinkedIn ADS campaigns, content to generate traffic and attention towards your page.

6. I will explain how to use Robotic Process Automation to spend even less time in generating new business opportunities and ensure that you can focus on what is most important, that is, close more negotiations and manage your business better.

7. I will explain how to conclude more negotiations through the straightline methodology

8. Finally, I will provide you with a series of tools that I myself use every day

---

1.2 Who's this book for?

This book is for all **people who want to generate new business opportunities**, people who realize that spending hours and hours calling a list of off-target contacts, today is an absolute waste of time, money and effort. In fact, we can count on tools (one of which is LinkedIn) through which you can get in touch with the right people at the right time.

These are both free and paid tools that allow you to generate new leads in target and then to be able to make appointments with people who we are sure they have an interest in the product / service, whether it is an application, a consulting service or an e-commerce.

In short, it is for all those people who seek **B2B** collaborations and partnerships (Business to Business) but also, to a lesser extent, for those who promote **B2C** firms (Business to Client).

This book is NOT meant to be a manual that sells smoke, in which unreachable goals are promised and readers are deceived to multiply their turnover by X times.

It is intended to be a summary of the **strategy that I myself as a marketing consultant and digital entrepreneur actually developed**, tested and improved over time to reach new customers and to promote my business, but also to bring value to the companies with which I have collaborated during these years.

My **goal is to make it possible for everyone to take advantage of the LinkedIn platform**, which in my opinion is amazing.

So ultimately this book is aimed at all those people who find it difficult to get new customers on LinkedIn, to those people who have a low response rate to their messages, to those people who are not at all experts in using this platform and who want to learn how to make the best use of all the available tools.

1.3 About Us

This Book is the result of a collaboration between me, **Matteo Romano** and my friend **Hassan Elfadul**, who I met during my Master program in Madrid, Spain.

Matteo Romano

I am a marketing consultant, Italian from Bergamo and currently based in Madrid, a wonderful, international and avant-garde city.

You will ask, how did you move from Bergamo to Madrid? It was certainly a sum of factors that led me to make this decision, the first of which certainly was to undertake a **Master in International Business at the EAE Business school**. My university career instead consists of a Bachelor Degree in Economics and Management at the **Bocconi University of Milan**.

For some time now Madrid has been my home and my job has been to provide help, technical support and advice to entrepreneurs, small and medium-sized companies, through my experience in the Digital Marketing sector.

I can resume my skills as follows:

Advertising: I dedicate to the creation marketing campaigns through all the main Social Medias (Facebook, Instagram and LinkedIn), Search engines (Google and Bing), Push notifications platforms (PropellerAds) and the Amazon Advertising platform.

Web Design: I design and develop e-commerce, websites and blogs (Wordpress, Shopify)

SEO: I position websites in Search Engines, researching keywords and working on the on-page and off-page optimization

Social Media Management: I create content (video, images, blog posts etc.) and post it to grow audience and brand awareness of Social Media pages (LinkedIn, Facebook, Instagram, Pinterest, etc.)

Consulting: I help you structure Marketing strategies to position your brand. **This consulting activity is my passion and my hobby** and I admit that many times talking to my family and my closest friends I consider myself very lucky to have this opportunity. Being able to define your job as a hobby is a luxury that some people manage to have but many don't. It is an activity that amuses me, that spurs me every day to give more and to deal with challenges in a sector where competition is at the highest levels.

Hassan Elfadul

I am a testing Engineer, Podcaster, world citizen but a proud Sudanese.

I am very grateful for this great opportunity and for the people I have met who surround me and help me improve and give more.

I have had the opportunity to live in different countries around the world, from my home **Sudan** to **Saudi Arabia**, then from **Malaysia** where I obtained my bachelor degree to where I am living now, beautiful **Spain**, where I was able to gain more knowledge in different areas and also obtaining my master's degree in **Project Management** .

You might wonder why there is an **engineer/podcaster** in the "About us" section of a Business related book! Well, this book is a project between Matteo and I, as he is the content creator of this amazing work, I am the one **designing and executing** this book for you. I also contributed by providing my view on the content of this book as a normal reader who is looking to improve their business on a platform as **LinkedIn**.

I believe our different perspectives and set of skills will deliver a book that is suitable and convenient to a bigger crowd of business owners who can always find so many great **tips and hacks** that can be applied directly to their businesses.

No more talk, now I would like to introduce you to the following section which will touch all the fundamentals that you need to manage on LinkedIn to position yourself as an expert in your sector, attracting business opportunities that were previously not possible.

CHAPTER:2
THE BASICS
FIRST

2.1 Your Personal Profile

Welcome to the second chapter, in which I will guide you in optimizing your personal profile, I will help you to understand and brush up on the concepts of Buyer Persona, and I will introduce you to LinkedIn segmentation tools.

But let's start from the beginning. The process of optimizing your LinkedIn profile includes these fundamental points (as an example, I have checked **Neil Patel's profile**, SEO expert founder of Neil Patel Digital):

Profile photo

The profile photo must be a professional, serious photo, which does not mean that it must be in a suit and tie and formal, but a photo in which you see your face directly because it is known that people, especially in Mediterranean cultures, appreciate seeing the person with whom you are talking to (in this case digitally, but the concept is the same). So, take a close-up photo, perhaps with a beautiful smile and without background noise (i.e. without distracting elements that can divert the viewer's gaze from your face). We know that the first impact is a fundamental aspect, so take my advice seriously, because it will help you in the future.

Title

The second factor to optimize is the title and the brief introductory phrase that says to the whole world "I am X, I deal with Y and I am unique because Z". For example, in my LinkedIn profile you can see that I am a "Marketing Consultant, marketing is about sharing your passion". This in my opinion is a description that fully represents me and above all communicates the passion that I put into my business every day.

In this section I advise you to go into details of who you are as a professional. First of all I ask you to spend some time for a captivating introduction that summarizes in a few lines what you do, where you come from, maybe if you have a family, what are the main skills that distinguish you and what are the main goals you have achieved in your career. Then use bullet points to detail your specific skills and the tools you can use. Finally, make your personal contact available to your audience so that anyone can contact you directly through email or mobile phone.

About

I am a New York Times bestselling author. The Wall Street Journal calls me a top influencer on the web, Forbes says I am one of the top 10 marketers, and Entrepreneur Magazine says I created one of the 100 most brilliant companies. I was recognized as a top 100 entrepreneur under the age of 30 by President Obama and a top 100 entrepreneur under the age of 35 by the United Nations.

I've helped Amazon, Microsoft, Airbnb, Google, Thomson Reuters, Viacom, NBC, Intuit, Zappos, American Greetings, General Motors, and SalesForce grow through marketing.

My marketing blog generates over 3 million visitors per month (51% of them spend money on paid ads), my Marketing School podcast generates over 1 million listens per month, my YouTube channel about marketing has over 20 million views and half a million subscribers, I have 960,000 Facebook fans, and 343,000 Twitter followers.

I've spoken at over 310 conferences and companies around the world. From speaking at Facebook and Thomson Reuters to every major growth marketing conference, I'm available and interested in speaking at events worldwide.

For speaking opportunities, collaborations, events, and business development, please email Grant Lingel (grant@neilpatel.com).

Featured

It is one of the most recent functions released by LinkedIn, where you can select the posts that have been most successful in your news feed, send your potential customers back to your website and promote an article you have written or images that are relevant to your audience.

Experience

In the section of work experiences I absolutely recommend adding the roles covered during your work experiences and, the objectives achieved, the skills necessary to fill this role and how long you have held that role.

Experience

Co-Founder
Neil Patel Digital
Oct 2017 – Present · 2 yrs 8 mos
Greater San Diego Area

Growing companies through innovative digital strategies.

Co-founder
Crazy Egg
Jan 2006 – Present · 14 yrs 5 mos

Crazy Egg is an analytics software that allows website owners to see what visitors are doing when they visit your site through "heatmaps" of visitor's clicks.

Education

In this section I strongly recommend that you indicate what your level of education is, whether it is high school, university degree or a PhD and also indicate which institution was the one that issued the certificate. This allows you to improve your personal brand and position yourself better than the competition.

Education

California State University, Fullerton
BA, Marketing
2003 – 2007

Skills

When you strive to position yourself on LinkedIn and attract potential customers, the keywords you use, play an important role, since the internal Linked search engine will show your profile exactly to the people that are looking for you.
For example, I have included in my profile all those keywords related to marketing activities, Instagram or Facebook campaigns, website development, my expertise in brand development, ecommerce management, etc.

Skills & Endorsements

SEO · 99+

Endorsed by **Nitin Manchanda, who is highly skilled at this**

Online Marketing · 99+

Endorsed by **Dennis Yu and 228 others who are highly skilled at this**

Endorsed by **Victor Motricala (mutual connection)**

Web Analytics · 99+

Endorsed by **Hiten Shah and 80 others who are highly skilled at this**

Endorsed by **Victor Motricala (mutual connection)**

Recommendations

In this section I advise you to ask your work colleagues, your boss and even your university professors to write a review for you regarding your skills, your uniqueness and also highlight the experiences they had with you in the professional environment. It may seem stupid but your profile will be much more professional and recommendations from other people is one of the most effective marketing tools since the beginning of the world.

Recommendations

Received (27)   Given (15)

Pramod Yadav
Digital Marketing Expert
(SEO PPC SMO)
February 16, 2019, Neil was
senior to Pramod but didn't
manage directly

Neil Patel is an astounding proficient, who brings the majority of the abilities and skill in digital marketing brand the board, content promoting and web-based social networking showcasing.

Mario Peshev
CEO @ DevriX - Hiring
Developers
December 23, 2018, Mario
worked with Neil but at
different companies

Neil has been my go-to resource for all sorts of digital marketing, SEO, content strategy, community building, and brand development through free content. His content was absolutely instrumental to my professional growth, scaling my agency from 25 to 40+, refining my inbound marketing strategy, a... See more

2.2 Your Ideal Customer

Once the optimization of your personal profile has been carried out and I am sure that in the coming months you will see the benefit, the time has come to create what is called a **customer persona.**

If your business is already launched and solid, surely you know what I'm talking about but if you are launching your new service or your new product you will surely hear about it often and I recommend you implement what is called the customer persona. **It will help you understand who exactly your client is**, what he expects from you, what is the type of content he appreciates and what are the values he shares with you. It is an absolutely fundamental tool also for the use of LinkedIn and for the strategies that we will explain later.

First of all: **What are customer personas?** These are **fictitious and generalized descriptions that represent your ideal client.** These representations help us in our marketing strategies, product sales and service and are therefore extremely useful.

Very often especially when you're working on a very innovative product or service, experts recommend that you carry out **interviews** with a group of people potentially interested in your idea in such a way as to ask them questions that go not only to answer the question "**Do these people need my service?**" but also to understand better what are the weak and strong points of your business idea.

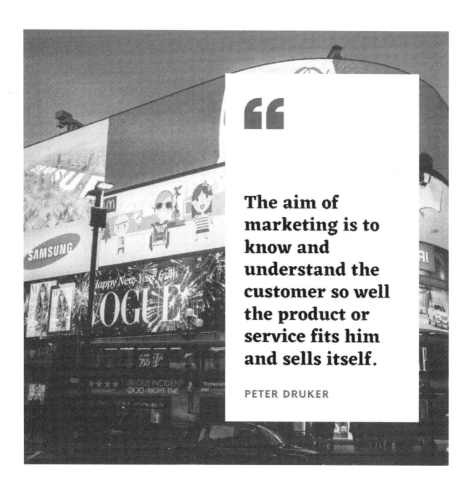

> ❝
>
> **The aim of marketing is to know and understand the customer so well the product or service fits him and sells itself.**
>
> PETER DRUKER

Below I list for you a series of questions that you can use to build a customer persona:

What is the role you play and the title?

What competences and skills are necessary to carry out your role?

What tools do you use in your work?

What is the size of the company?

What are you responsible for?

What is your educational background?

What was your career path?

What are the challenges that distinguish your role?

How are the objectives that are set for your role measured?

How old are you?

In which industry and sector do you work?

Are you married? Do you have children?

What I have just reported are general questions, but I advise you to make them more specific because you will receive detailed answers and solve your doubts.

Persona buyer template

PERSONA NAME:	Sample Sally	SECTION 2: WHAT?
GOALS *Primary goal? Secondary goal?* ⑤	• Keep employees happy and turnover low • Support legal and finance teams	
CHALLENGES *Primary challenge? Secondary challenge?* ⑥	• Getting everything done with a small staff • Rolling out changes to the entire company	
WHAT CAN WE DO *...to help our persona achieve their goals?* *...to help our persona overcome their challenges?* ⑦	• Make it easy to manage all employee data in one place • Integrate with legal and finance teams' systems	

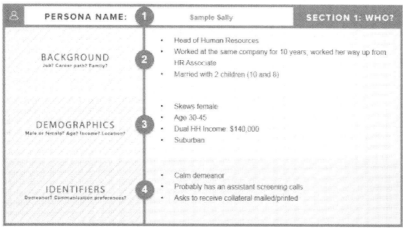

PERSONA NAME: ①	Sample Sally	SECTION 1: WHO?
BACKGROUND *Job? Career path? Family?* ②	• Head of Human Resources • Worked at the same company for 10 years, worked her way up from HR Associate • Married with 2 children (10 and 8)	
DEMOGRAPHICS *Male or female? Age? Income? Location?* ③	• Skews female • Age 30-45 • Dual HH Income $140,000 • Suburban	
IDENTIFIERS *Demeanor? Communication preferences?* ④	• Calm demeanor • Probably has an assistant screening calls • Asks to receive collateral mailed/printed	

PERSONA NAME:	Sample Sally	SECTION 4: HOW?

MARKETING MESSAGING
How should you describe your solution to your persona?

(10)
- Integrated HR Database Management!

ELEVATOR PITCH
Sell your persona on your solution!

(11)
- We give you an intuitive database that integrates with your existing software and platforms, and lifetime training to help new employees get up to speed quickly.

PERSONA NAME:	Sample Sally	SECTION 3: WHY?

REAL QUOTES
About goals, challenges, etc.

(8)
- "It's been difficult getting company-wide adoption of new technologies in the past."
- "I don't have time to train new employees on a million different databases and platforms."
- "I've had to deal with so many painful integrations with other departments' databases and software."

COMMON OBJECTIONS
Why wouldn't they buy your product/service?

(9)
- I'm worried I'll lose data transitioning to a new system
- I don't want to have to train the entire company on how to use a new system.

2.3 Understanding B2B Clients

Once you have created the template of your ideal customer persona, you will be able to understand who the person you are contacting is, how to communicate with him, what are his needs and therefore you would be ready to generate leads and potentially sit at the negotiating table to sell your product or service.

But, first of all, I would like to dive deeper into the characteristics of a B2B customer and of B2B sales:

- B2B customers are normally very focused on understanding the logic of the product

- The decision of a B2B customer normally includes a process that consists of several steps which normally includes the joint decision of more than one person

- Usually the sales process is long.

- The process of purchasing a B2B product or service requires the establishment of a relationship of trust and mutual respect between the seller and the buyer, in which the seller often finds himself in the role of external consultant, advising and guiding the buyer to ensure that he benefits from the potential of the product

- In marketing relating to the sale of B2B services or products, the Brand is created through personal relationships and sales through consultancy

"

Here's my whole marketing idea: treat people the way you want to be treated.

GARTH BROOKS

2.4 LinkedIn Advanced Search

Now that you have clear who's your customer and how he purchases, I'd like to dive into the LinkedIn Advanced Search tool, the **instrument that allows you to segment your target of potential customers in a very detailed way.**

Through the Buyer persona you already know who your ideal target, and to convert this into LinkedIn results, you should focus on these questions:

1. In which sector does my ideal customer work?

2. In which city / region does he live? Does he work locally? Nationally? Internationally?

3. What is his job title? And what's his seniority level?

4. Is he a 1st, 2nd or 3rd level connection in LinkedIn?

P.S. if you're not sure about what LinkedIn connections are and how they work, check the following.

What are 1st, 2nd and 3rd connections in LinkedIn?

1st-degree connections

People you're directly connected to because you've accepted their invitation to connect, or they've accepted your invitation. You'll see a 1st degree icon next to their name in search results and on their profile. You can contact them by sending a message on LinkedIn.

2nd-degree connections

People who are connected to your 1st-degree connections. You'll see a 2nd degree icon next to their name in search results and on their profile. You can send them an invitation by clicking the Connect button on their profile page, or by contacting them through an InMail. Learn more about InMail.

3rd-degree connections

3rd-degree connections - People who are connected to your 2nd-degree connections. You'll see a 3rd degree icon next to their name in search results and on their profile.

If their full first and last names are displayed, you can send them an invitation by clicking Connect.

If only the first letter of their last name is displayed, clicking Connect isn't an option but you can contact them through an InMail.

Example: your ideal customer is a Digital Marketing Manager who lives in the US, who's a 3rd Connection and who works in the Marketing & Advertising Industry

1. Go to the top Search Bar and type "**Digital Marketing Manager**". Once done, go to click

on "Search all results for "Digital Marketing Manager"

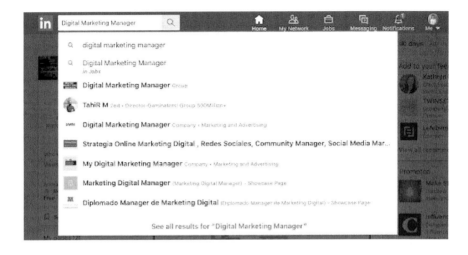

2. You will get this screen

3. Click on "**All Filters**" and you'll get this screen

4. Here you will select connection "**3rd**", location "**United States**", industry "**Marketing and Advertising**"

5. And here we go with the list of potential customers that you can connect with!

Now you know how to segment your customer persona through LinkedIn and you're ready to apply the Strategy that I have used to convert 15% of contacted people into potential customers!

But first, I have selected for you a series of titles that can help you in selecting your customer

Job Titles

Marketing Job Titles	
Marketing Specialist	Copywriter
Marketing Manager	Media Buyer
Marketing Director	Digital Marketing Manager
Graphic Designer	ecommerce Marketing Specialist
Marketing Research Analyst	Brand Strategist
Marketing Communications Manager	Vice President of Marketing
Marketing Consultant	Media Relations Coordinator
Product Manager	Public Relations
SEO Manager	Social Media Assistant
Content Marketing Manager	Brand Manager

Administrative Job Titles	
Administrative Assistant	File Clerk
Receptionist	Account Collector
Office Manager	Administrative Specialist
Auditing Clerk	Executive Assistant
Bookkeeper	Program Administrator
Account Executive	Program Manager

Branch Manager	Administrative Analyst
Business Manager	Data Entry
Quality Control Coordinator	Project Manager
	Administrative Manager
Office Assistant	Chief Executive Officer
Secretary	Business Analyst
Office Clerk	Human Resources
Risk Manager	

C –Level Job Titles

CEO — Chief Executive Officer	CMO — Chief Marketing Officer
COO — Chief Operating Officer	CHRO — Chief Human Resources Officer
CFO — Chief Financial Officer	CDO — Chief Data Officer
CIO — Chief Information Officer	CPO — Chief Product Officer
CTO — Chief Technology Officer	CCO — Chief Customer Officer

Leadership Titles

Team Leader	Supervisor
Manager	Superintendent
Assistant Manager	Head
Executive	Overseer

Director	Chief
Coordinator	Foreman
Administrator	Controller
Controller	Principal
Officer	President
Organizer	Lead

Top Information Technology (IT) Job Titles

Computer Scientist	Computer Programmer
IT Professional	Network Administrator
UX Designer & UI Developer	Information Security Analyst
SQL Developer	Artificial Intelligence Engineer
Web Designer	
Web Developer	Cloud Architect
Help Desk Worker / Desktop Support	IT Manager
	Technical Specialist
Software Engineer	Application Developer
Data Entry	Chief Technology Officer (CTO)
DevOps Engineer	
	Chief Information Officer (CIO)

Sales Job Titles

Sales Associate	Account Executive
Sales Representative	Account Manager

Sales Manager

Retail Worker

Store Manager

Sales Representative

Sales Manager

Real Estate Broker

Sales Associate

Cashier

Store Manager

Area Sales Manager

Direct Salesperson

Director of Inside Sales

Outside Sales Manager

Sales Analyst

Market Development Manager

B2B Sales Specialist

Sales Engineer

Merchandising Associate

Construction Job Titles

Construction Worker

Taper

Plumber

Heavy Equipment Operator

Vehicle or Equipment Cleaner

Carpenter

Electrician

Painter

Welder

Handyman

Boilermaker

Crane Operator

Building Inspector

Pipefitter

Sheet Metal Worker

Iron Worker

Mason

Roofer

Solar Photovoltaic Installer

Well Driller

Business Owner Titles	
CEO	Administrator
Proprietor	Director
Principal	Managing Partner
Owner	Managing Member
President	Founder

Positions in a Company	
Board of Directors	Human Resources
C-Level or C-Suite.	Accounting Staff
Shareholders	Marketing Staff
Managers	Purchasing Staff
Supervisors	Shipping and Receiving Staff
Front-Line Employees	
Quality Control	Office Manager
	Receptionist

Customer Service Job Titles	
Virtual Assistant	Customer Service Manager
Customer Service	
Customer Support	Technical Support Specialist
Concierge	Account Representative
Help Desk	Client Service Specialist
	Customer Care

	Associate

Operations Manager	Operations Director
Operations Assistant	Vice President of Operations
Operations Coordinator	
Operations Analyst	Operations Professional
Continuous Improvement Consultant	Scrum Master
	Continuous Improvement Lead

Finance and Accounting Job Positions

Credit Authorizer	Financial Analyst
Benefits Manager	Finance Manager
Credit Counselor	Economist
Accountant	Payroll Manager
Bookkeeper	Payroll Clerk
Accounting Analyst	Financial Planner
Accounting Director	Financial Services Representative
Accounts Payable / Receivable Clerk	
	Finance Director
Auditor	Commercial Loan Officer
Budget Analyst	Bookkeeper
Controller	Accounting Analyst
Credit Authorizer	Accounting Director

Benefits Manager	Accounts Payable / Receivable Clerk
Credit Counselor	Auditor
Accountant	Budget Analyst
	Controller

Engineering Job Titles

Engineer	Mining Engineer
Mechanical Engineer	Nuclear Engineer
Civil Engineer	Petroleum Engineer
Electrical Engineer	Plant Engineer
Assistant Engineer	Production Engineer
Chemical Engineer	Quality Engineer
Chief Engineer	Safety Engineer
Drafter	Sales Engineer
Engineering Technician	Biological Engineer
Geological Engineer	Maintenance Engineer

Researcher / Analyst Job Titles

Researcher	Biostatistician
Research Assistant	Title Researcher
Data Analyst	Market Researcher
Business Analyst	Title Analyst
Financial Analyst	Medical Researcher

Teacher Job Titles

Mentor	Preschool Teacher
Tutor / Online Tutor	Test Scorer
Teacher	Online ESL Instructor
Teaching Assistant	Professor
Substitute Teacher	Assistant Professor

Artistic Job Positions

Graphic Designer	Novelist / Writer
Artist	Computer Animator
Interior Designer	Photographer
Video Editor	Camera Operator
Video or Film Producer	Sound Engineer
Playwright	Motion Picture Director
Musician	Actor
Director of Photography	Music Producer

Healthcare Job Titles

Nurse	Dental Hygienist
Travel Nurse	Orderly
Nurse Practitioner	Personal Trainer
Doctor	Massage Therapy
Caregiver	Medical Laboratory Tech
CNA	Phlebotomist

Physical Therapist	Medical Transcriptionist
Pharmacist	Telework Nurse / Doctor
Pharmacy Assistant	Medical Laboratory Tech
Medical Administrator	Physical Therapy Assistant
	Massage Therapy

Hospitality Job Positions

Housekeeper	Cruise Ship Attendant
Flight Attendant	Casino Host
Travel Travel Agent	Hotel Receptionist
Hotel Front Door Greeter	Reservationist
Bellhop	Events Manager
Cruise Director	Meeting Planner
Entertainment Specialist	Lodging Manager
Hotel Manager	Director of Maintenance
Front Desk Associate	Valet
Front Desk Manager	Concierge
Porter	Group Sales
Spa Manager	Event Planner
Wedding Coordinator	

Food Service Job Titles

| Waiter / Waitress | Cafeteria Worker |
| Server | Restaurant Manager |

Chef	Wait Staff Manager
Fast Food Worker	Bus Person
Barista	Restaurant Chain Executive
Line Cook	

Scientist Job Titles

Political Scientist	Geologist
Chemist	Physicist
Conservation Scientist	Astronomer
Sociologist	Atmospheric Scientist
Biologist	Molecular Scientist

On-the-Phone Jobs

Call Center Representative	Dispatcher for Trucks or Taxis
Customer Service	Customer Support Representative
Telemarketer	
Telephone Operator	Over the Phone Interpreter
Phone Survey Conductor	Phone Sales Specialist
Mortgage Loan Processor	

Counseling Job Positions

Counselor	Guidance Counselor

Mental Health Counselor	Social Worker
Addiction Counselor	Therapist
School Counselor	Life Coach
Speech Pathologist	Couples Counselor

Cosmetology Job Titles

Beautician	Makeup Artist
Hair Stylist	Esthetician
Nail Technician	Skin Care Specialist
Cosmetologist	Manicurist
Salon Manager	Barber

Writing Job Titles

Journalist	Columnist
Copy Editor	Public Relations Specialist
Editor / Proofreader	
Content Creator	Proposal Writer
Speechwriter	Content Strategist
Communications Director	Grant Writer
Screenwriter	Video Game Writer
Technical Writer	Translator
Social Media Specialist	Film Critic
Ghostwriter	Copywriter
	Travel Writer

Physical Labor Job Positions

Warehouse Worker	Physical Therapy Assistant
Painter	Housekeeper
Truck Driver	Landscaping Worker
Heavy Equipment Operator	Landscaping Assistant
Welding	Mover

Other Job Titles

Archivist	Translator
Actuary	HVAC Technician
Architect	Attorney
Personal Assistant	Paralegal
Entrepreneur	Executive Assistant
Security Guard	Personal Assistant
Mechanic	Bank Teller
Recruiter	Parking Attendant
Mathematician	Machinery Operator
Locksmith	Manufacturing Assembler
Management Consultant	Funeral Attendant
Shelf Stocker	Assistant Golf Professional
Caretaker or House Sitter	Yoga Instructor
Library Assistant	

CHAPTER:3

THE 15% CONVERSION RATE LEADGEN STRATEGY CRLS

3.1 The results I have achieved

So here we are now in the third chapter, the one in which I will explain to you **step by step** what strategy I applied to convert my **marketing plan** into a real success. All the factors that we have been mentioning in the second chapter that mainly concern the optimization of the profile and your personal brand, will directly impact the results that you could achieve by applying this strategy.

Why?

Because the **credibility** factor of your personal brand comes out when your potential customer visits your personal profile. If he finds himself in front of a meager profile, with little information, careless and unprofessional, the chances that you will have to receive an answer will be very low because you will not be credible in his eyes. On the other hand, a **curated profile**, which **tells a story**, your story, explains **who you are, what you do and how you do it**, will give you **much higher chances of sitting at the negotiating table** with him.

During these years of using LinkedIn tools and optimizing the strategy that I am about to explain I successfully achieved very satisfactory results. On average of each 100 people I contact, at least 15 of them responded back to me by sending their contact information such as phone numbers or email addresses.

The strategy's results:

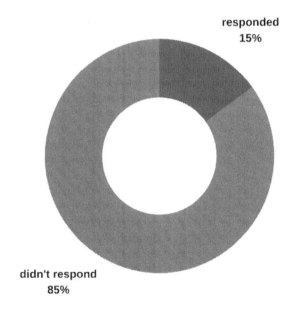

responded
15%

didn't respond
85%

This result is based on some of the fundamentals of marketing and sales:

1. Go straight to the point.
2. Create a connection between you and the contact person.

3. Position yourself as an authoritative and credible person.
4. Use a friendly tone.
5. Provide a punctual solution that solves a problem
6. Preferably ask open questions.
7. Generate a need, create a state of anxiety
8. Create a feeling of scarcity

Through these pillars of communication and psychology, anyone can become an effective seller.

Never forget that you only have one opportunity to make a first impression – with investors, with customers, with PR, and with marketing.

NATALIE MASSENET

What is the strategy I used?

1. I **studied** the characteristics of **my main customers** in detail.

2. I identified an ideal target customer.

3. I used LinkedIn's segmentation tools to identify how many people I could reach.

4. I developed **various message alternatives (templates)** that I tested to check which one was the most efficient. For example I have discovered that those Long, Boring messages that you receive everyday have a very low conversion rate. So, we should go straight to the Point!

5. I used **AB testing tools** and the kanban model to keep track of the progress of my tests by following these parameters:

   A. Answer rate: every 100 messages sent, how many responses do I get?

   B. Conversion rate: every 100 messages sent, how many contacts do I gather?

C. Meetings rate: of those contacts gathered, how many do schedule an appointment with me?

D. Sales rate: of those appointments scheduled, how many do convert into customers?

6. I identified the best times during which my target replied most frequently (during the morning hours, around 8 - 9 AM)

7. **I kept track and reinvigorated the curiosity** of those people who had not replied to my messages, by contacting them again and making the best use of my time and effort spent on lead generation

8. I used **automation tools** to make faster and more scalable the strategy

9. I have used **LinkedIn's paid tools** to further expand my user base and know their characteristics even better.

All these points, if summarized in a concise manner, give shape to what it is called a **funnel which basically consists of a model that summarizes all the steps necessary to convert an unknown person into a potential customer.**

3.2 The 15% Conversion Rate Funnel

This is the most important chapter of the book. As mentioned, I will talk about the funnel used as a roadmap, where the concept is that the more people enter your funnel, the more you know your audience and the better you become in addressing their pain points. Time and efficiency will train you to convert more contacts into customers.

The LinkedIn 15% Conversion Rate

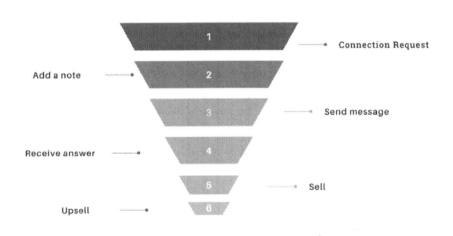

FUNNEL:

Remember the example of the Digital Marketing Manager we mentioned in the previous chapter? Let's say that I want to contact **Trov Pan, Digital Marketing Manager in New York City.**

1. **Click on request**

As you have seen through the segmentation tool of LinkedIn, the platform provides you with a pool of users to contact. The first step is precisely to go on the list of contacts and click the Connect button. Then a window will open in which you can decide whether to add a note or send the message now.

2. **Add a note**

This step is essential to personalize the message through which you contact the person. In this section you can either use your personal message or use one of the TEMPLATES I HAVE PERSONALLY USED THAT I HAVE SUMMARIZED STARTING FROM CHAPTER 3.3.

Click on the send invitation button and proceed with the next candidates.

Invite Trov to connect   ✕

Build a quality network by connecting only with people you know.

Message (optional)

Ex: We know each other from...

300 / 300

▓ PREMIUM

Don't know Trov? Send an InMail with Premium to introduce yourself. More people reply to an InMail than a connection request.

Reactivate for Free

Cancel   Send invitation

3. **Receive a reply**

Once you have contacted the first bunch of users, you will realize right away if the template used is effective or you need a pivot.

4. Schedule a meeting

Once you get a reply, don't lose time and move to the next step by scheduling a meeting.

5. Sell

This is the point I like most because it is the moment when you have to sell, whether you are on the phone or you are in a face to face meeting with the reference person, in the following chapters you will be able to access a series of key skills that will lead you to improve your sales strategy.

6. Upsell

If you are good enough to conclude one or more negotiations and your customer is satisfied with the service or product offered, it will be time to make him a long-term customer and then sell him other products or services.

Now that you have had access to the specific strategy to convert 15% of people contacted into potential customers, it is time to move on to the next phase that is the templates to use for your first contact messages.

3.3 Template 1: The Pain Point

Target: 1st degree contacts

Goal: address the pain point

Message

Hey [prospect],

could you send me your phone number where I can directly contact you? I have noticed that you still don't rank in Google My Business [pain point], which is an opportunity I believe you shouldn't miss.

Thank you!

Best, [Your Name]

3.4 Template 2: Appropriate Person

Target: 1st degree contacts

Goal: addressing the appropriate person to talk to

Hey [prospect],

I'm writing in hopes of finding the appropriate person who handles [department]. In my company we are selecting some partners for [solution] and I'd like to see if you'd match our criteria and reach [goal].

Thank you!

Best, [Your Name]

3.5 Template 3: 2nd Degree Connections Introduction

Target: 2nd degree contacts

Goal: asking for an introduction to the 2nd degree connection through a 1st degree connection

Message

Hey [prospect],

It was great chatting with you last week. Like we talked about, you mentioned it might make sense for me to connect with [2nd degree contact]. I'm sure you have a lot going on right now, so I went ahead and attached a quick message below to make the introduction as easy for you as possible. With that said, would you be able to make the introduction for me here?

Thanks!

Best, [Your Name]

3.6 Template 4: 2nd Degree Connections Name Dropping

Target: 2nd degree contacts

Goal: using leverage from a 1st degree connection without asking for an intro.

Hey [prospect],

could you send me your phone number where I can contact you directly? I have noticed that you still don't rank in Google My Business [pain point], which is an opportunity I believe you shouldn't miss. Thought it might make sense for us to talk.

But if not, who do you recommend I talk to?

Thanks, [Your name]

3.7 Template 5: Group members

Target: members of a group

Goal: address the members of a group

Message

Hey [prospect],

I saw we are both members of [insert group] and thought it might make sense for us to talk. I have noticed that you still don't rank in Google My Business [pain point], which is an opportunity I believe you shouldn't miss.

Could you send me your phone number where I can directly contact you?

Thanks! [Your name]

3.8 Template 6: News Feed

Target: members of a group

Goal: address the members of a group

Hey [prospect],

[insert statement reference context from LinkedIn News Feed]. I have noticed that you still don't rank in Google My Business [pain point], which is an opportunity I believe you shouldn't miss.

Could you send me your phone number where I can directly contact you?

Thanks! [Your name]

3.9 Template 7: Events

Target: people who've been featured in special events or articles

Goal: asking for contact info

Message

Hey [prospect],

congratulations on being featured in XXX. I have noticed that you still don't rank in Google My Business [pain point], which is an opportunity I believe you shouldn't miss.

Could you send me your phone number where I can directly contact you?

Thanks! [Your name]

3.10 Template 8: Follow up

Target: Follow up with customers who didn't respond

Goal: Re-engage

Message

Hey [prospect],

I haven't heard back from you last week. It makes sense to talk, let me know how your calendar looks.

If not, who is the appropriate person to talk to?

Thanks, [Your name]

3.11 Template 8: No answer

Target: Reestablishing a new communication with a costumer who has not answered

Goal: Re-engage

Message

Hey [prospect].

I wanted to follow up about helping you increase [unique value] If it still makes sense to talk, let me know what your calendar looks like.

Thanks, [Your name]

3.12 Template 9: Schedule Meeting Follow Up

Scenario 1: if the prospects responds positively and with a specific time

Message

Hey [prospect],

great hearing from you. I just sent over a calendar invite for this Thursday at 11:30 am with my conference line attached to it. If you have any questions in the meantime or if there are any changes in scheduling, feel free to send me a note.

Talk soon, [Your name]

Scenario 2: if the prospects responds positively but without a specific time

Hey [prospect],

Great hearing from you - Here are a couple of times that work for me this week:

- [Day 1]
- [Day 2]

Go ahead and pick a time that works best for you as well as the best number to reach you at and I'll give you a call then.
But if none of these times work for you, let me know what does and I'll work around your schedule.

Thanks
[Your name]

3.12 A/B Testing and Kanban model

One of the most used techniques implemented by marketing people to check the results of their products/services is the one of split testing, also called A/B testing. **A/B Testing** consists in **offering different versions of the same product at different groups of customers at the same time.** By observing the changes on the behavior of customers, you can immediately measure the impact of the different variations. For example, email marketing was the pioneer of this technique.

Let's use an **example**, let's consider that you want to send three of the different templates that I have provided in chapter 3 to three different groups of people through LinkedIn. The total number of people over which you want to test the results of the templates is 300, you will have to send the first message to 100 people, the second to 100 people and the third to the last 100 people.

The way you can measure the quality of the templates is by checking the conversion rates that you get, consisting, in this case, in:

How Many People	viewed your message but didn't reply
	viewed and the replied to your message
	viewed, replied and provided their contact information

So, with the A/B test technique you can measure the results by structuring a chart in this way:

	Viewed	Replied	Contact info
Template 1	90%	15%	7%
Template 2	85%	6%	3%
Template 3	80%	5%	1%

What you can conclude with this table is that the template number 1 is the most effective because 90% of people viewed the message, 15% replied and 7% of them provided their contact information.

This kind of table that allows you to keep track of the results of your A/B tests and to make scientific decisions, guided by the collected information.

These kinds of experiments are very efficient when we need to learn, test and validate some experiments and it's a principle called **Lean Manufacturing, invented by The Japanese car manufacturing company Toyota.**

According to the lean methodology, you have to **keep track of the variations** of your product segmenting them by variations to do, in progress, ended and validated (successful tests that have proved their results).

You can follow the Lean Methodology by using the following table. Every column can have maximum 3 projects at the same time

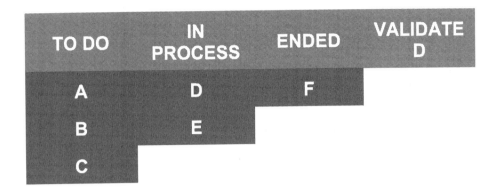

TO DO	IN PROCESS	ENDED	VALIDATED
A	D	F	
B	E		
C			

You start working with project A. D and E are in process. F is waiting for validation.

TO DO	IN PROCESS	ENDED	VALIDATED
G		D	F
H	B	E	
I	C	A	

You have validated F. D and E are waiting for validation. G, H and I are new projects that wait to be started. B and C are in process. A has ended its testing phase.

TO DO	IN PROCESS	ENDED	VALIDATED
	G	D	F
H→	B→	E	
I→	C→	A	

B and C have been completed, but in the kanban model, they cannot advance towards the following columns up to the moment in which A, D and E have been validated. You cannot start working on H and I unless you free up space in the next columns.

CHAPTER:4

SKYROCKET YOUR LEADGEN STRATEGY

4.1 LinkedIn Ads

Now that you know how to use LinkedIn's free segmentation tools and how to apply the Ledagen strategy that I have used, in this section we will talk about **how to create advertising campaigns through LinkedIn Advertising Manager** which is the tool that allows you to reach even more potential customers through paid campaigns.

I personally believe it is a great tool because it allows you to AB test different audiences and creatives (images, texts used and Call to Actions) through the settings that we will go through now.

In order for you to create a LinkedIn campaign, you need to go to the LinkedIn campaign manager and create a new account. Once you have done so, click on the button create campaign.

Campaign Objective

Once created a new campaign, you have to select which is your campaign objective.

Awareness

This kind of objective needs to be selected by companies who are young or not widely known and want to reach more people by promoting their brand and tell everybody " we are X and we do Y"

Consideration

This kind of objective is for those companies that want their target audience to perform a specific action like clicking on the website link, engaging with the post created or viewing a video.

Conversions

This campaign is dedicated to those companies that need to either generate leads, reach new customers or ask them to perform a website conversion like for instance filling in a contact form or downloading their free PDF and for those companies who are looking for new employees.

Location

One very important factor of a successful advertising campaign is the geographic targeting. Some people believe that targeting a very broad and geographically wide audience is better than being precise. Well, they're wrong! You will have a much more precise advertising campaign and better results if you are more precise..

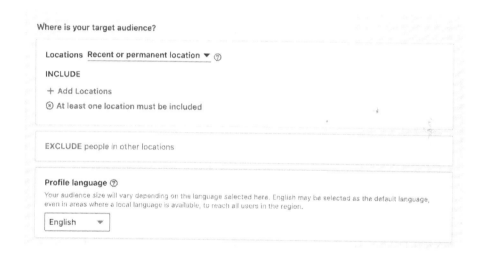

Audience

This is a crucial factor for a successful advertising campaign because here you would be able to segment properly your target audience. If you have already worked on your buyer persona it would be easier for you to already figure out who you are addressing and what the characteristics are of the company or person that you're looking for.

Company

In this section you can select which kind of company you want to target whether it is a small company, a medium-sized company or a Fortune 500 company. You can also segment by growth rate, the industry in which it works, the company name and the company size.

1. **Company** Category

2. **Company** Connections

3. **Company** Growth Rate

4. **Company** Industries

5. **Company** Names

6. **Company** Size

Demographics

In this section you can select the age and gender of the person you want to reach.

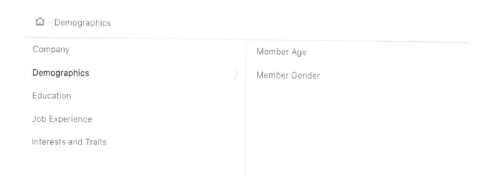

Education

In this section you can filter by the level of education, the school attended and the field of education of the person you want to reach out to.

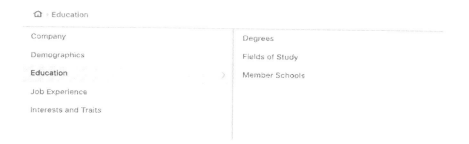

Job Experience

In this section you can filter by job experience, functions, seniority level, title, skills, years of experience and interests (traits of the person you want to reach out to).

1. **Job** Functions

2. **Job** Seniority

3. **Job** Titles

4. **Member Skills**

5. **Years of Experience**

6. **Interests and Traits**

Interests and traits

In this section you can specify which are the interests and traits of your target audience.

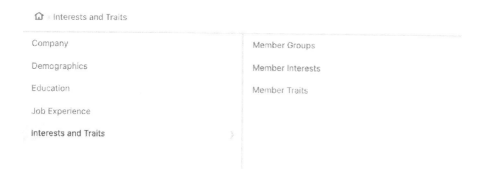

Ad format

You can choose from a variety of ad options like a single image, a carousel image, a video, a text, a spotlight, a message and a conversion ad.

Placement

In this section you can choose if you want to advertise directly on the LinkedIn platform or in their partners' websites as well.

Placement

LinkedIn Audience Network ⑦
Reach up to 25% more of your target audience by running your ads on LinkedIn and our partner apps and websites.

☐ Enable the LinkedIn Audience Network

ⓘ The LinkedIn Audience Network is not currently available for the objective or ad format you selected.

Conversion Tracking

In this section you can select your conversion tracking Analytics. For example you can track how many people click on your campaign link, how many scroll down 75% of your landing page and how many fill in the contact form and download the free PDF.

Conversion tracking (optional) ⑦

Measure the actions members take on your website after clicking or viewing your LinkedIn ad.

+ Add conversions

Budget & Schedule

In this section you can decide which is your advertising budget and for how long you want to

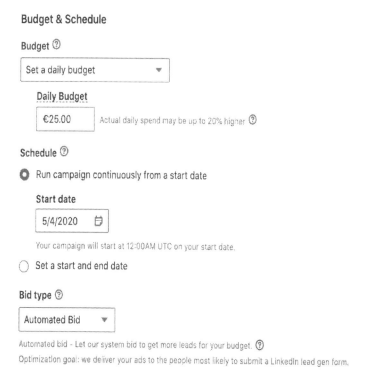

place it and spread it throughout time.

Once you have setup the campaign, on the right panel you'll be able to see the forecasted results provided by LinkedIn that indicates:

1. **Your** target audience size.

2. **The** budget **available.**

3. **The** maximum potential expenditure.

4. **The** potential impressions generated

5. **The average expected** click-through rate

6. **The** potential clicks generated.

4.2 Creating a Company Page on LinkedIn

LinkedIn, unlike other social media platforms such as Facebook, is specifically dedicated to companies and for this reason it is highly advisable to create a business profile that can help you increase your brand awareness, position yourself as an expert and get more leads.

If you haven't yet thought about creating a company page for your business on LinkedIn, it's time to do it!

My advice to you is first of all to invite professionals who you already know and people who work in your sector. They will be more open to visit your company page and like it.

How to create a LinkedIn Page?

1. Go to the left panel of LinkedIn and click on Create new page.

2. Fill in the Page Identity section.

3. Fill in the company details.

4. Add your logo and describe briefly your company.

5. Preview and publish!

What kind of content should you post?

I highly recommend you to independently develop an editorial calendar and write content, post reference images, share articles in newspapers or other authoritative platforms.

In fact, unlike other social media platforms, **LinkedIn** is a platform solely dedicated to professionals and companies, therefore, as it is not so popular with the general public, it is **easier to compete and generate a specific audience**.

The advantages of having a LinkedIn page are indisputable but certainly those companies that are constantly present and post relevant content for their audience have an undoubted **competitive advantage** over the other players on the market.

In fact it is to be considered that the your followers on LinkedIn will most likely be interested in your services and therefore generating B2B partnerships will be easier.

Before wondering what content to post, it is important to structure an **editorial calendar** that respects the needs of your target audience: on LinkedIn people and professionals are active on average throughout the week and in particular during the mornings.

Usually **between 9 and noon are the times** in which more engagement is generated and in which it is easier for your content to be visible.

Why? Precisely because **professionals are most likely active during these hours** and it is specifically during the morning that they are looking for new collaboration and take care of expanding their partnerships.

As I've already mentioned, if you are in a position to do it, I advise you to **create content at least three times a week**.

> **Everyone can benefit from seeing smart marketing.**
>
> LEWIS HOWES

Saturdays and Sundays, on the other hand, are days during which it is not convenient to post and during which the engagement is very low, therefore on Saturdays and Sundays dedicated to resting or refreshing your strategies for capturing new customers.

Social Media Calendar

LinkedIn				
Hour	Title	Copy	Images	Link
9 AM				
3 PM				
9 PM				

Facebook				
Hour	Title	Copy	Images	Link
9 AM				
3 PM				
9 PM				

Instagram				
Hour	Title	Copy	Images	Link
9 AM				
3 PM				
9 PM				

What kind of content?

On LinkedIn the contents that generate the most engagement are:

- Brand Storytelling

- Video Case Studies

- Business Introduction Videos

- Behind the Scenes or How Things Are Made

- Infographics

- Updates and Business Events

- Meet the Team

- Answering an Industry Question

- FAQS

Therefore, in summary, I advise you in the best case scenario to post every day and as you can see there is no shortage of material to create and generate engagement, it is only a matter of brainstorming, creating and doing.

4.3 Driving traffic using Articles and Blog Posts

Another great way to reach out to new potential customers or partners is to **generate unique and valuable content to address specific pain points of your target audience through Blogs**.

We have talked in advance about the utility of having an editorial calendar and posting content constantly, but one of the most important features of LinkedIn is for sure the possibility of writing articles directly in the platform and redirect **backlinks** to your own independent website.

As some of you might know, generating Backlinks is a very powerful SEO skill that helps you position yourself higher in search engines and get more traffic.

If you are not sure about what your target audience pinpoints are, I strongly recommend you to reach out to a keyword research tool or a professional in order to **research the keywords people are using** when looking for the product or the service that you provide.

This keyword research will also allow you to know more about your target audience and here's a **list of Keyword research tools** you can use:

1. Ubersuggest

2. Spyfu

3. SEMRush

Let's see now **how to understand more about your potential customer through Keywords**. Let's use an example: If you are promoting **dental operations**, you will discover that the main concerns of your target audience are:

- The pain associated with the dental operation.

- The consequences of the anesthetic.

- The examples of before and after successful dental operations.

- The best dental doctors in their country.

With a keyword research tool, creating very specific and pain-solving articles and blog posts is going to be very easy.

In fact if you already know in advance what the main concerns of your potential target audience are then it is going to be easier to lower their barriers and create an opportunity for you to sell your product or service.

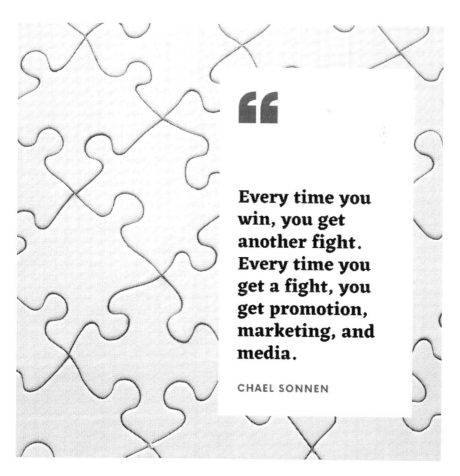

Every time you win, you get another fight. Every time you get a fight, you get promotion, marketing, and media.

CHAEL SONNEN

4.4 Creating a LinkedIn Group

LinkedIn groups consist of a great tool to **create engagement and community** around people who share the same industry interests, and look for the same answers, the post and view jobs, who won the great business contacts and establish themselves as industry experts and Leaders.

Being an active participant in a group can help you and your business network with other professionals and businesses in your field, especially those who are outside of your immediate circle of current and present colleagues, competitors and fans.

As a business, creating a LinkedIn group will be your **direct connection to your customers** and will help you use displacement to create a space where your audience can ask questions and connect.

But remember, lending groups are in places where businesses eschewed continuously bomb their potential customers with advertisements.

It is a place of communication and the place of professionals to establish authentic relationships.

Moreover, lending groups can help you boost your **Brand's name and authority** so I strongly recommend you to look for groups relevant to your business as starting gauging with their content, their posts and their members.

Once you have started engaging with members of that group, you can start promoting your own content as well, this can help you generate leads and it is also a great way to bring more traffic to your website.

How to join a LinkedIn Group?

In order to join a LinkedIn group you can either search for groups by name or keywords or browse for groups recommended for you by LinkedIn.

Just go to the interest bar at the top of your homepage and choose groups; click Discover at the top of the page to see your suggested groups; request membership by clicking "Ask to join" button.

How to start a LinkedIn Group?

If you are willing to create your own Lending Group, on your homepage go to your interest button

1. On your homepage, hover over the left bar and click on Groups.

2. Click on Create New Group.

3. Add Name, Description, Industry, Rules Discoverability and Permissions.

How to use LinkedIn Groups?

Once you've created your LinkedIn group one of your main duties is to encourage engagement.

You can do so by:

- Recognizing members and liking or commenting on the content they share

- Using the Manager's Choice feature to pin a discussion to the top of your Group and highlight the issues that are most relevant to your audience

- Linking your quality group discussions to your other social media channels to encourage new voices and contributions to your discussions

Also remember these following tips in order to create even more engagement:

- Ask specific questions.

- Pay attention. Stay tuned to what others are saying

- Stay on topic. Always make sure your posts and discussion points are relevant to your Group

How to use LinkedIn groups to generate leads?

You can make a list of potential customers by using LinkedIn groups search functions and filter by job, title, company, geography location. With this list of prospects, you can send personalized and free direct messages to those people and build a connection.

You can make a list of potential customers by using LinkedIn groups search functions and filter by job, title, company or geography location. With this list of prospects, you can send personalized and free direct messages to those people and build a connection.

In conclusion, LinkedIn Group is the perfect space where you can grow, build and place yourself as the industry leader with your online community both from a personal standpoint and a business perspective.

CHAPTER:5

LINKEDIN ROBOTIC PROCESS AUTOMATION (RPA)

5.1 What is Robotic process Automation "RPA"?

Robotic Process Automation is a technology that allows us to setup a software (a robot) that emulates the actions of a human within digital systems to perform a task or process.

Robotic Process Automation robots utilize the user interface to get data

and perform actions exactly as a human would do. They interpret, trigger responses and communicate with other systems in order to perform on a vast variety of repetitive tasks.

The most important thing is that robots never sleep and don't make any mistake at all!

Most importantly, the costs to automate a previously human-performed task is extremely low and robots can leverage the productivity of the tasks that you want to automate. Cost efficiency and compliance are no longer operating costs but a byproduct of the automation.

What tasks can RPA robots perform?

1. Login into any app.

2. Connect to APIs.

3. Copy-paste data.

4. Move files.

5. Extract information from any file.

6. Read and write databases.

7. Open emails.

8. Scrape data online.

9. Make calculations.

What are those processes that can be automated with RPA?

Robots can automate basically any high-volume, repeatable processes that qualify for automation. **With RPA you can easily and rapidly implement automation tasks, skyrocket your productivity and achieve ROI as never before.**

"

Automation is good, so long as you know exactly where to put the machine.

- BILL GATES

5.2 Why implementing RPA automation in your marketing strategy

What are the business benefits of RPA?

Robots are here to stay. The faster you harvest their potential, the faster you create a competitive edge for your business. Robotic Process Automation delivers direct profitability while improving accuracy across organizations and industries. Enabling RPA to handle any processes will not only transform and streamline your organization's workflow. It will allow for **superior scalability and flexibility within the enterprise**, doubled by fast, tailored response to specific needs. Software robots are easy to train and they integrate seamlessly into any system. Multiply them, and instantly deploy more as you go.

They constantly report on their progress so you can go even bigger and better by using operational and business predictability, while improving strategically.

Better accuracy	Robotic Process Automation software robots are programmed to follow rules. They never get tired and never make mistakes. They are compliant and consistent.
Once instructed, RPA robots execute reliably, reducing risk. Everything they do is monitored. You have the full control to operate in accordance with existing regulations and standards.	Improved compliance

Fast cost savings	RPA can reduce processing costs by up to 80%. In less than 12 months, most enterprises already have a positive return on investment, and potential further accumulative cost reductions can reach 20% in time.
Across business units and geographies, RPA performs a massive amount of operations in parallel, from desktop to cloud environments. Additional robots can be deployed quickly with minimal costs, according to work flux and seasonality.	**Extremely scalable**

| Increased speed and productivity | Employees are the first to appreciate the benefits of RPA as it removes non-value-add activities and relieves them from the rising pressure of work. |

5.3 Recommended LinkedIn Robotic Process automation tools

During these years I have been using one RPM software to automate LinkedIn and it's called LinkedHelper, with which you can automate:

- LinkedIn Sales Navigator
- LinkedIn Recruiter (Full & Lite)
- Get thousands of targeted contacts by sending personalised invitations to 2nd & 3rd contacts
- Auto-mailing system, Auto-Responder, Sequential Messaging to 1st connections or LinkedIn Group Members
- Automatic Profiles Visiting & Export to CSV file (Google Sheets / MS Excel)
- Build targeted mailing list
- Boost your profile and get hundreds of endorsements from other users in no time
- Invite 1st connections to join a LinkedIn Group
- Endorse your contacts automatically to get endorsements in return

- Automatically add your signature to messages
- Automatically follow or un-follow LinkedIn connections
- Automatically withdraw sent pending invitations (invites canceller)
- Powerful Lists manager - allows to build your own lead generation funnel and avoid intersections between campaigns

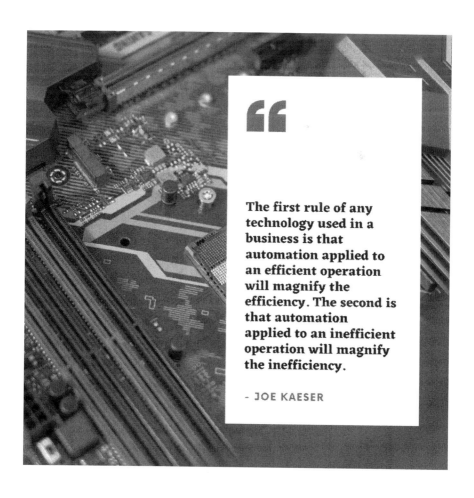

> The first rule of any technology used in a business is that automation applied to an efficient operation will magnify the efficiency. The second is that automation applied to an inefficient operation will magnify the inefficiency.
>
> - JOE KAESER

CHAPTER:6

HOW TO USE PERSUASION TO SELL MORE - THE STRAIGHT LINE

6.1 What is straight line persuasion?

And here we are in the 6th chapter! In this section of the book I will try to explain to you some **advanced techniques in order to persuade and influence people so you end up SELLING MORE!**

This methodology has been invented by **Jordan Belfort** and we all know about him through the amazing interpretation of **Leonardo di Caprio in The Wolf of Wall Street.** I am sure you will think "oh, yes I remember that crazy drug addict tricking people selling them garbage stocks!"

But wait! Don't Jump to conclusions

If this guy was capable of selling garbage stocks to both professionals and non-professional people, it means he was doing something good!

What?

Elevating a sale process and making it a masterpiece is a work of art! Now you're with me, aren't you?

I have been studying his method and I can guarantee you that it works!

But let's start from the beginning: Jordan called his system Straight Line Persuasion because just as the shortest distance between any two points is a straight line, you are trying to take a customer from 1-10 and get them to buy or sign **as quickly as possible** without any wasted time.

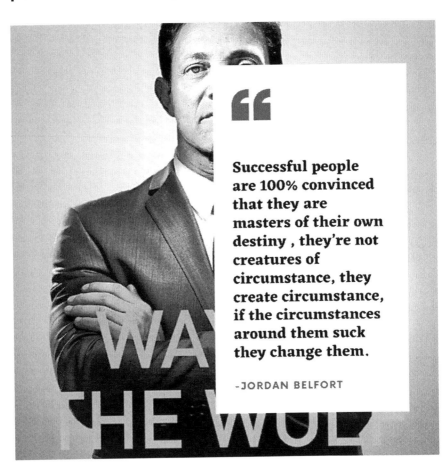

"

Successful people are 100% convinced that they are masters of their own destiny , they're not creatures of circumstance, they create circumstance, if the circumstances around them suck they change them.

-JORDAN BELFORT

6.2 The pillars of the Straight Line Persuasion

The Straight Line Persuasion is based on 3 main pillars:

1. **Developing a relationship** with the customer, where he feels that you perfectly know him and you're his friend. This will build a strong bond leading to gaining the customer's trust.

2. **Asking specific questions** to get his attention and understand his specific needs (also called pain points in the marketing terminology)

3. **Controlling the sale by keeping it on the straight line**, that means when the conversation gets away from your main focus - the sale -, you need to bring it back on the straight line

6.3 Buyers vs. Non-buyers

So, as a salesperson your main objectives are to:

1. **Find the right people to speak to** (and we've addressed this part in the previous chapters, so you should have all the necessary tools to do so through LinkedIn).

2. **Immediately identify those people who are neither relevant nor interested** in your product/service.

Remember that you should **never treat your buyer as if he**:

Didn't know you or the **product** you're selling

Shouldn't be buying, because he needs what you're selling

Can't afford your product

The goal isn't to convert non-buyers into buyers, but to CLOSE every CLOSEABLE POSSIBLE DEALS.

You should be concerned when the buyer decides to purchase from someone else instead of you. This means that you're missing something either in your presentation or in your product/service, which means you have to focus on it and make it better.

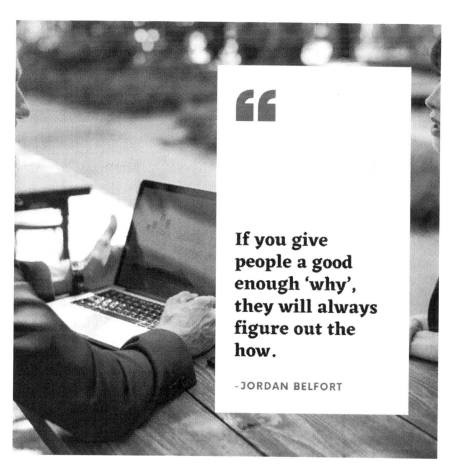

> If you give people a good enough 'why', they will always figure out the how.
>
> -JORDAN BELFORT

You can assume in any given room of **100 people**:

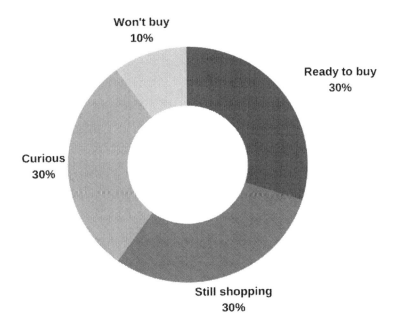

- **30 are ready to buy right now. These are people who know they have to make a decision quickly and are motivated to buy now.**

- **30 are still shopping** but are motivated to buy.

- **30 are curious,** "just looking", maybe they'll buy today, maybe they'll buy tomorrow, they're not in a rush

- **10** were dragged there by someone else, they don't want to be there and they will never buy from you.

One more thing: if you need to make a war, you can't go without a helmet, without guns and without being trained. **You need a plan, You NEED a script**. This is non-negotiable. No matter how good you are. It needs to be customized to suit your particular field. It needs to be memorized and you need to be able to read from it without sounding like you are reading from it (like a great Hollywood actor).

This is important: you have to memorize the script and know it so well that the customer doesn't understand you're using a script: **if the customer knows you are reading from a script you are done.**

6.4 Cold calling: 4 things you must establish in 3 seconds

When you cold call someone you can be anyone you want to be, but you only have 3 seconds to establish 3 things. You are:

Enthusiastic as hell.

Sharp as a tack.

An expert/authority figure (People want to work with the expert, the top guy/girl in the field that can help them to achieve their goals and take control of their life)

Tonality

One of the most important elements of a successful salesman is **TONALITY**. When it comes to influence and persuade, your tonality is crucial, because through tonality you can make people feel specific emotions and by leveraging emotions you close deals. **People buy on emotions, not on logic!**

That's why when you are speaking to someone, you should sound as a friend, don't say you care, just imply it with your tonality. **You should sound**:

- Trustworthy

- Empathetic

- Caring

Important tonalities

- Scarcity/Secret (quiet, hushed tonality). If you want someone to listen to you YELL. But if you want someone to REALLY LISTEN to you *whisper*. By lowering your voice and whispering, you imply you have a secret, something scarce.

- Certainty: Most people don't have a sense of certainty so if you do people will listen

- Disarming

6.5 How NOT to build rapport with your customer

One of the biggest mistakes most salespeople make when trying to develop rapport with their customers is that they talk about their hobbies/interests.

Wrong!

When a customer starts talking to you about their holiday in New Zealand you don't start talking to them about that and go off into no man's land.

Instead of talking to the customer about their hobbies and interests (or anything else irrelevant to the sale) **you build rapport by demonstrating that you are an expert and a person that can help them to achieve their** goals.

Remember why you are talking to a customer. You are there to make money. You are there to close a deal. You are there to sell. That's it. You can talk about their holiday or go out for a drink AFTER the sale is made but not now.

How to sell a pen

One of the most famous scenes in *The Wolf of Wall Street* movie is when Jordan asks his stockbrokers to "sell me this pen." But no one seemed to know how to do it.

Neither did I.

"

Sell me this pen!

-JORDAN BELFORT

I learnt the secret however by watching an interview on YouTube in which Piers Morgan asks Jordan how to do it and Jordan said that the biggest **mistake** most salespeople make when trying to sell a pen (or anything else) is that they try to sell you on the benefits and features of the product:

"This pen is great!"
"This pen is the best!"
"This pen can write upside down!"

One thing I have understood from this: do NOT try to sell a product by listing the benefits and features of it!

I believe the best way to sell anything Is by asking your customer specific questions in order to understand his purchasing strategy.

For example if you're selling a LinkedIn Lead generation software, I would ask you: How many leads do you get now every month? How many would you like to achieve?

This way I would already know which features of my Leadgen software strengthen and propose you to achieve your goals through my exclusive product. Easy! **I am solving a specific problem.**

6.6 How to close the deal

Let's draw conclusions: How do you close the sale?

1. The customer must LOVE your product. They must think that your product will solve the problem they have, and your product should provide exactly this!

2. The customer must TRUST you and your company. Since you've developed a trust relationship with your customer, he must feel confident to get in touch with you anytime for anything

3. The customer must know that you LISTEN to his future needs

If your customer says no, it's for the following reasons:

- He isn't convinced your product is the best, so it must be improved.
- He doesn't trust you & your company.

Overcoming objections

In case your customers isn't convinced yet, he will surely have objections like:

- I can't afford it.
- I need to think.
- This is bad timing.
- My wife will kill mc.
- I need to speak with my wife.
- I've been burned before.

However **90%** of objections are just stall **tactics**.

When someone says *"I need to speak with my wife"* or gives you any other objection it's a stall tactic because:

- They're not convinced logically
- They're not convinced emotionally
- It's a question of money
- They have a negative belief to buying

PS: **The best time to overcome objections is BEFORE they come up**

CHAPTER:7
CONCLUSION

Here we are at the end of this book which turned out to be a real challenge that helped me and my colleague Hassan to **push our limits a little further** and raise the bar of our quality of teamwork. This book is the result of a huge effort in terms of organization, planning and implementation.

In particular Hassan's skills in terms of **project management** are a clear example of how **organizational** and **critical ability**, combined with a good component of **creativity** and **ambition**, can lead to completely exceptional results. I speak of exceptionality because this book, written, designed and launched during a very short period of time, that is, about a month, makes me **very proud** and I am sure that it is the same for Hassan too.

During this period, in fact, not only have we strengthened our friendship which was already solid and often led us to discuss our vision of the world, the business to which we are both very close, and ourselves, but we also laid the foundations for a long-term professional partnership, because sharing time on a common project always involves new challenges. These challenges in particular concern the **quality of communication**, the ability to **respect** each other and **listen** to **criticism**. So it implies the need for a **mature** and very **pragmatic** collaboration.

In this book we have given our best to explain what the foundations for creating your personal brand are through LinkedIn improving the quality of your profile; we then deepened the issues related to your customers to your target audience and those skills necessary to understand who you need to contact and how to reach these people. we also explained step by step What is the suitable strategy to generate business opportunities in a simple and scalable way, using analytical measurement tools and laying the foundations for a long-term sustainable business; we then talked about how the results of this strategy can be increased exponentially through the use of LinkedIn marketing campaigns, the creation of professional company profiles, the use of LinkedIn groups aimed at generating leads; finally we went to deepen the great topic of online and off-line sales, inspired by Jordan Belfort who knew how to achieve exceptional results through strategies planned from the beginning and through a rhetorical ability, persuasion and use of the word out of the ordinary .

Hassan and I hope that this book is useful to all those who want to **launch themselves** into the world of LinkedIn and in the professional use of this incredible tool but also to all those who already have the experience in this regard and hope to achieve even more results through our advice from the world of work.

I want to end by thanking first of all you readers who have trusted us in buying this book. Then, **I would like to personally thank my family**, my mom and my dad who have always been a stimulus for me and have always invited me to take my responsibilities, to launch myself into my sometimes bizarre projects and always believe in my ideas. I also want to thank my **aunts** who are a great example to follow, as they bear those values of correctness, teamwork, motivation and a tireless desire to improve. I thank my **friends** who are always close to me even if sometimes geographically distant, because they always give me ideas of self-criticism and are always open to constructive discussion for the good of all. I would like to thank all those **professors** I met during my journey both during my university career at the Bocconi University of Milan and in the master's degree in International Business at the EAE Business School in Madrid. Finally, I would like to thank all the work **colleagues** that I have had the honor of knowing during my career that they have pushed me to give more and do better, teaching me that taking care of interpersonal relationships is the foundation of everyday life.

I hope we will have the opportunity to meet again to talk about business,

Good luck

Matteo

CHAPTER:8
REFERENCES